Dissecting

Aisha Wade

BookLeaf
Publishing

Dissecting my soul © 2022 Aisha Wade

All rights reserved.

Presentation by *BookLeaf Publishing*

Web: www.bookleafpub.com

E-mail: info@bookleafpub.com

ISBN: 9789357695213

First edition 2022

I dedicate this book to my daughter Jasmine a true princess by nature. I hope this inspires you to always listen to your heart and understand that women deserve to be loved and treated with respect ALWAYS. Also, to mummy's boy Junayd, the only man in my life that lights the way forward with his endless love and protection. I love you both dearly, you are truly gods greatest blessing.

ACKNOWLEDGEMENT

I would firstly like to thank my mother for always being my biggest rock and teaching me how to be a strong independent woman. The endless love and support from you and Shaun have got me through my darkest days. Also, my big sister Lara for being that stand in mum whenever I needed her to be. She has always been there for me, allowing me to be my crazy, emotional erratic self and still love me all the same. This book is for everyone that believed in me as a writer and poet. Thank you for your patience.

PREFACE

I originally started writing poetry in my mid to late 20, s. I was medically diagnosed with PTSD and anxiety 4 years after my daughter was born. I then suffered a major breakdown at the age of 26 just before my son was born, after also enduring many years of domestic violence. Through lots of different support and therapies, I started to voice my feelings through Poetry, and I found that this coping mechanism has helped me to process my traumas. I write from opening up my heart and bearing my soul.

RED

A bright, yet deep sometimes.........dark concept.
A heart full of love if you accept.
Something sexy, seductive and/or warm....
....a heart bleeds RED if it is torn.

The colour "je t'adore."
Dangerous to some that don't live by the law.
Explore the concepts behind the colour RED,
Expressed so differently, 'tis a colour don't be misled.

Gripped by sensation
REDS common denomination; expressed & associated by a whole nation
Love, danger & blood is the RED that we know,
RED can mean anything daring to show.

I WRITE MY LOVE

If the pen in my hand controlled my thoughts.....
Then I would write all the emotions I know I've
been taught,
Although the pen doesn't feel what's inside,
It tries to express all the stories I've cried.
The thoughts although silent, are voiced by the
pen,
It seems easy to write when I think over and
over again
And flows so easily when I connect to my heart,
A blank piece of paper is all I need to start.
Please take my pen and hold it for some time.....
Then scratch your own heart please.....you'll find
a sign, to write your love

'INNERVOICE'

A voice can tell you to do things
sometimes good
Sometimes bad
Another voice within me
sounds so terribly sad
It's trying to speak
But just can't get the words out
Little voice please tell me
What you're all about
OK I hear you
'Now why are you so sad?'
Please stop telling me things
That sound so bad

So, you're the voice
Thats been nagging at me
Telling me to give up
Walk away and be free
Now I understand
And thank you for speaking out
Thankyou! for giving me a voice

Now I can shout.

DREAM OR NIGHTMARE LIMERICK

Next time you ask me 'Why do you cry?'
Look into your soul and you tell me why,
You can't see your own heart 'cos bad things are
in the way,
Yet I'm the one to blame is what you always say,
How can I love you? Someone lost in a
nightmare,
When all I do is dream of the love we could
share,
You still fight with me, say I'm the excuse your
hearts bad,
I will take the blame, 'coz I'm good, I love you
and that's why I'm sad.

ANOTHER LOVE POEM

Sometimes you're bitter in love, because you
hurt,
Thats why you turn from this page....
...Not another poem about love!
Each line being like a stamp of rage.

How could your audience possibly understand?
That it helps to write the anger
Expressed by the pen in your hand.

Everyone knows the pain of love,
A story told over & over again,
But sometimes it can be different,
When loves an understanding to gain.

SOULLESS

It is in a human the immaterial and spiritual part,

That I certainly believe 'cos I had one at the start,

The soul is a machine, a driving force within you,

How can I function? Now you've taken mine too.

I don't understand why mine hasn't made you good

It's a soul worth keeping, if you don't believe me...you should!

Now there's nothing left inside, just a long story to tell,

And without my own soul I'm an emotionless shell.

C O N T R O L

Who has the remote
To turn me on?
And where has all the colour
In my life gone?
I've become so dull
And ohh so black & white
Get off my remote
I don't need it tonight.
I am here,
I exist right in front of your face
Not so easy to C O N T R O L
You say is the case.
Do you think...you can just
Flick the buttons, do as you say
I'm not the TV
On re-set...EVERYDAY!

HIM

He makes me think and makes me lie,
Why do I let HIM make me cry?
Its HIM that makes me do wrong?
When his words fall so sweetly off his tongue.
To commit this this crime is such a sin...
...but I can't help myself...it is just HIM.

Sometimes I long to be by his side,
...feel his every touch, endure and abide,
He makes me feel good, I'm sure its HIM I truly
love
I want to tell the world how I'm trapped in this
love song
But ashamed of what I'm doing...it's just so
wrong.

I can't help myself he is my addiction,
Am I feeling the truth or is this all just fiction?
He makes it seem real with his every touch on
my skin,
It is all his fault...it is simply just HIM.

WHEN THE GLOVE FITS
(the theory of love)

How do you know when love is true?
Can you turn a few potions into something blue?
There is no science or tested theory of love
'Tis in each individual...
Created by a power up above.

Who is that person, if one was so true?
Is it just a saying when you say 'I do?'
Why do we express love in such different ways?
Cry, laugh and shout.....
Even Shakespeare wrote plays

So next time you ask;
How do you know love is true?
Just ask the other person 'Do you love me too?'
There is no science or tested theory of love,
When the find the right one
The'll fit like a glove.

WHY???

Inside you can't see my heart asking 'WHY?'
'WHY?'.......you choose to make me cry?
I suppose you're not the one to blame.
So, I choose to let myself accept the pain.
'WHY?'......why are your ways just so totally wrong?
I have accepted this for far too long,
Now is the time to say goodbye......my hearts a slow beat,
I feel no love......'WHY?'

There's no ground at my feet

SKY OF EMOTIONS

Sky, tell me what you feel,
Rain, drown me with your tears,
Sunshine, show me some colour,
Grey clouds take you away....
Make my life duller.

Snow, warm me up, keep me safe inside,
Everything's turned to ice,
All the flowers have died.
Like the sky and its moods,
I'm forever changing,
Try and stay warm and bright forever,
Keep my moods from re-arranging...
Changes

FORBIDDEN FRUIT

Even when I try not to love you.... I do!
My hearts, no longer a part of me,
It controls itself and that you can't see
Because I am me, but my heart is you
It's not my fault, but its everything you do
I'm a person with no heart, but still exist
YOU took my heart, but MY love persists.
I don't want it back, you've kept it too long,
Forbidden fruit, sour on my tongue

IMPRINT

EXCUSE ME! CAN YOU WASH MY BRAIN?
YOU REMOVED IT, ABUSED IT....NOW I
SEE A STAIN,
MARKED WITH YOUR IMPRINT....YOU
DID THIS TO ME,
TAKE IT BACK & CLEANSE IT, LET MY
BRAIN BE FREE.

TELL ME WHY YOU DID THIS TO MY
MIND....PLEASE?
ITS MINE, ITS PRECIOUS....EACH &
EVERY LITTLE PIECE,
IT HELPS ME DEICDE THE RIGHT
CHOICES TO MAKE,
HOW CAN I CHOOSE NOW? IVE BEEN
BRAINWASHED FOR GODS SAKE!

....SO YOU STOLE MY HEART & STAINED
MY BRAIN,
I CANT FUNCTION NORMAL ....HAVE I
NOW GONE INSANE?

BROKEN

Like a candle,
You lit the way
And without a word
You just blew me away.
When darkness fell,
I could see no lights,
All I was left with:
Dark lonely nights
You were the light
That guided me through....
Broken silence,
Broken thoughts,
Broken....because of you.

EMPTY PLATE

You will never see the good that I do,
Your blinded by devils and don't have a clue,
Not until you clean up the mess in your own
heart,
I am wasting life's time....and have from the
start.
Good things always come to those who can wait,
I am hungry for happiness....still an empty plate.
You have filled me with pain....my heart aches
so much,
Lovings' not an emotion I can feel in your touch,
Your fighting my love like instead it is hate,
Im not giving up....
I DEMAND! Love on my plate.

DEVILS & ANGELS

As I shout and cry, I become weak,
Why does my life seem so bleak?
Standing alone the world looks so dark,
While all around me devil's lark.
Playing with my mind like a stick in the fire,
Burning my soul calling me a liar

For why is it the devils are attracted to thee,
Can't they see the halos all around me?
Angels come and protect me with your wings
Guard me like a wall, destroy these evil things.
Things called hate, addiction and depression,
Take the devils away they're a sign of repression.

TEARS

Straight from the heart,
Like poison inside,
Cry, cry, cry
My emotions just died.
Why does it hurt to keep them locked away?
No one's listening to the things I have to say.
My hearts exploding, please let this poison out,
But fear takes over, what's this crying about?
Why do tears fall from the eye?
Maybe seeing is believing
.....and that's what makes you cry.
If I look deep into my heart
I can burst the bubble of fear,
.....then let my tear's part.

FINAL CURTAIN

Time to stand down
Let the show come to an end,
The plots been exposed,
So now I lose a friend

If we were acting,
....and the love wasn't true
Hasn't the time come,
To end it with you?

Now you know
We need to move on,
The timing is right,
But the loving is wrong.

We don't have to look,
At the damage we've caused,
Final curtain please!
....no standing applause

IF......IF I WERE INVISIBLE

I
I would......
I would float......
I would float to places that I secretly admire
......and watch,
watch over people......
with hidden desires
I won't make a fuss, you won't know I'm there,
Because to be invisible, nobody cares.
Floating around from place to place,
No expressions judged upon my face.
Oh! the possibilities,
Seem too tempting to resist,
Please make me invisible,
I long......not to exist!

10X SORRY

1. SORRY   I came into your life, became such a pain.

2. SORRY   for the secrets, the lies, such a game.

3. SORRY   I tried to please you but left you in doubt.

4. SORRY   I made you question love; it wasn't meant to freak you out?

5. SORRY? I could say it over & over & over again.

6. BUT......I'm going to keep saying sorry at least until I get to 10.

7. SORRY   for the good times and smiles that make you cry.

8. SORRY for making you question and ask why?why?why?

9. SORRY for being real but my love was never true.

10. SORRY I'm at number 10, sorry for not loving you.

Dissecting my soul

Take one look at me
Look deep, don't hide
Don't just look, cut me open
To reveal the inside.
Explore, investigate, most of all dissect
Use my heart as your guide
And you won't be upset.
Study me from the inside out,
Only then you'll know.
You should not have a doubt,
When with the scalpel you take each part
Remember the brains connected to the heart!
So be careful, be tender when you slice
As surgical dissection will suffice.
Unlike my heart at war with my brain
It's hard to separate blood from the vein,
When YOU play surgeon, I have no control,
But only I, MYSELF, ME can dissect my soul.

Milton Keynes UK
Ingram Content Group UK Ltd.
UKHW021839041024
449101UK00013B/871